KU-365-204

THE WAYS OF THE WOLF

Written by
SMRITI PRASADAM-HALLS

Illustrated by
JONATHAN WOODWARD

wren
&rook

For Gabe, Rafi, Tom and Ben – my pack – S.P.H.

For Mali and Samson, my two adventure-loving, creative cubs who inspire me every day – J.W.

First published in Great Britain in 2017 by Wren & Rook

ISBN: 978 1 5263 6030 4
E-book ISBN: 978 1 5263 6075 5
10 9 8 7 6 5 4 3 2 1

Wren & Rook
An imprint of
Hachette Children's Group
Part of Hodder & Stoughton
Carmelite House
50 Victoria Embankment
London EC4Y 0DZ

An Hachette UK Company
www.hachette.co.uk
www.hachettechildrens.co.uk

Publishing Director: Debbie Foy
Editor: Liza Miller
Designers: Claire Munday and Emily Bornoff

Printed in China

LIST OF CONTENTS

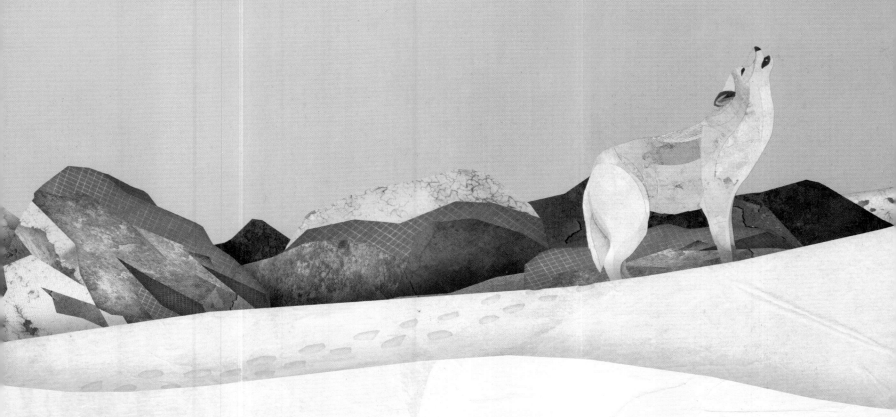

WOLVES IN OUR MIDST

Majestic and fierce, proud and strong, the wolf has always been a source of fascination – and fear. With speed, intelligence and impressive strength, the wolf is famed for its hunting skills and spine-tingling howl.

Yet the wolf remains one of the most misunderstood and misrepresented of all creatures. Holding a prominent place in the folklore of many cultures, it fills our fairy tales and our imaginations with menace and mystery, and is frequently cast as our mortal enemy.

The truth is that wolves and humans are more closely connected than we dare to admit. With a sophisticated code of communication, the deep-rooted bonds of love and loyalty within a wolf pack mirror our own family lives in many ways.

Sensitive or savage? Beautiful or bloodthirsty? You decide, as we uncover the wild and wonderful ways of the wolf ...

PACK LIFE

Nose-to-nose in tender greeting or mischievous play, the wolf pack demonstrates loyalty, warmth and affection in a shared family life. Hunting, travelling and living together, the pack's bonds run deep.

At the heart of the pack are the alpha male and female. Paired for life, they are a unit. Together they are responsible for the pack.

The rest of the pack are ranked with a higher or lower status according to their achievements in hunting or defence – although a forceful personality helps too.

The pups of the pack will join the social order when fully grown. Until then, they playfully compete to be the best. Once mature, many will leave home to search for new territory and to start new packs.

Whatever their age, whatever their status, the wolves work as one.

THE SECRET CODE OF WOLVES

Through postures, facial expressions and tail and ear positions, wolves can send silent, swift messages to each other. Sometimes a glance or a gesture is all that's needed to avoid a quarrel. In this way, rank and order are maintained; peace is restored.

ANGRY

Teeth bared and snout wrinkled; ears out low and to the side; tail straight out or raised.

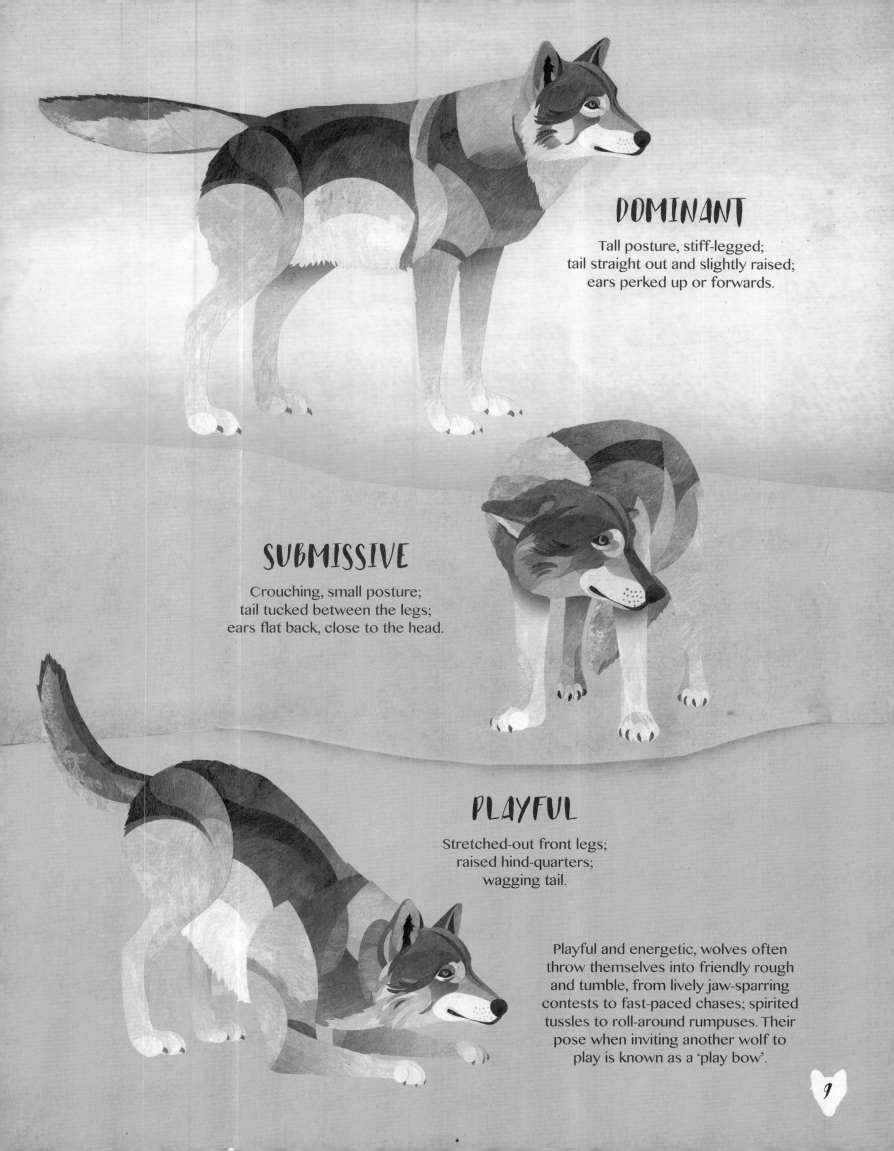

DOMINANT

Tall posture, stiff-legged;
tail straight out and slightly raised;
ears perked up or forwards.

SUBMISSIVE

Crouching, small posture;
tail tucked between the legs;
ears flat back, close to the head.

PLAYFUL

Stretched-out front legs;
raised hind-quarters;
wagging tail.

Playful and energetic, wolves often
throw themselves into friendly rough
and tumble, from lively jaw-sparring
contests to fast-paced chases; spirited
tussles to roll-around rumpuses. Their
pose when inviting another wolf to
play is known as a 'play bow'.

CALLS OF THE WILD

The haunting howls of a wolf pack can be heard from more than 10 kilometres away. Whether a call to gather the clan, an attempt to attract a mate, a cry for help or a song of mourning, the wistful howl of the wolf is unique and unmistakable.

Wolves communicate with all sorts of different sounds. Everyday whines and whimpers accompany playful family life. A defensive snarl or growl will warn away intruders and rivals. The dog-like bark, though seldom heard, signals imminent danger.

However, of all wolf cries, it is the heartrending howl that hangs in the night air, full of longing, echoing eerily.

SCENT OF DANGER

Rain has fallen and the valley is green and refreshed. The wolf pack picks up the scent of a herd of elks. They must still be some 2 kilometres away from here, but their path is mapped in the clues they have left behind.

The wolves pause, their long noses absorbing the story hanging in the air, on branches and on tree stumps. From scents, chewed leaves, muddy footprints and traces of skin, they piece together that the herd has slowed down. Their prey is tired, and one or two of the throng are struggling to keep up.

But wait – a different smell lingers here: another wolf. A rival has ignored the unmistakable scents that mark off their territory and has dared to trespass here. He has left his own scent, as distinctive to him as a fingerprint.

The pack howls collectively. There is no place here for an intruder.

13

THE SOUND OF SILENCE

A pine cone falls to the forest floor and a wolf pricks her ears. She senses movement long before it appears, her highly developed hearing able to receive almost silent messages across vast distances.

Moving her ears independently, she can turn towards noise, pinpointing the source of a sound and focusing her attention on it. Those patient ears – ever upright – capture sound even when she sleeps.

EYES OF AMBER

Smell and hearing may be used first, but sharp eyesight helps the wolf to detect the smallest of movements around him: the dart of a firefly; the twitch of a tail.

His bright eyes can recognise a known wolf from afar, quickly distinguishing between friend and foe, so that he may defend himself if the need arises.

Seeing as keenly in darkness as by day, travelling by night poses no problem to him. He moves effortlessly under a blanket of midnight blue, with only a sprinkling of stars for company.

CONQUERING THE ELEMENTS

The wolf is a master of adaptability. It survives in the most hostile habitats, protected and preserved by the natural features of its physique.

Arctic wolves, a subspecies of the grey wolf, have developed a dazzling coat of pure white that disguises them perfectly in their snowy habitat. Smaller ears and noses than other wolves mean they lose less heat, while a thick layer of body fat provides extra insulation. Most impressive of all is the ability to control their own body temperature.

TAIL

A long, bushy tail blankets the wolf's face when it lies down. This keeps it warm in temperatures of −70 °C and shields its eyes from dust and wind blowing across the tundra.

FUR

A double layer of fur keeps wolves warm and dry. Soft, short inner hairs trap heat next to the body, while thick, long outer hairs act as a waterproof, snow-proof coat. When spring arrives, the wolves shed much of their fur to keep cool.

CAMOUFLAGE

Wolf coats vary depending on the animals' surroundings, allowing them to blend in.

PAWS

Large, flexible feet can travel across any surface, gripping tightly to rocks and logs when chasing antelope up a steep incline and spreading weight evenly to walk across deep snow and thin ice. Claws prevent slipping when the wolves scramble across uneven ground.

THE WOLF FAMILY

When wolves weave their way into our consciousness, our culture and our stories, it is almost always the grey wolf that comes prowling into view. But the grey wolf is just one member of the family of wolves.

GREY WOLF

The grey wolf is the largest and most well-known member of the family.

RED WOLF

The red wolf is a little smaller than the grey wolf, sporting a fine coat of black or grey fur, flecked with red. Critically endangered not long ago, small populations have been reintroduced to the south-eastern USA.

ETHIOPIAN WOLF

The rust-coloured Ethiopian wolf is smaller and redder than the red wolf, but just as endangered. It can only be found in seven mountainous areas in Ethiopia.

EASTERN WOLF

The eastern wolf is also threatened, being confined mainly to one nature reserve in Canada.

18

COYOTE

The cunning and clever coyote is very similar to the grey wolf, although it only weighs a third as much. Coyotes are common across the majority of North America.

GOLDEN JACKAL

The golden jackal looks like a miniature grey wolf. It supplements its meaty diet by foraging for fruit and vegetables, and is found from eastern Europe to India and Thailand.

BLACK-BACKED JACKAL AND SIDE-STRIPED JACKAL

With fox-like features and slender build, the black-backed jackal and side-striped jackal complete the family of wolves.

FOUR-LEGGED FRIENDS

All dogs are closely related to wolves, although some are more wolfish than others. We need not fear the wolf in our home, though; domestic dogs can be tamed, while the wild wolf cannot.

LANDS OF THE WOLF

The wilds of the forest, the lonely mists of the mountain, the harsh heat of the desert and the soft snow of the Arctic have all, at one time, been home to the wolf.

NORTH AMERICA

SOUTH AMERICA

KEY

 Arctic wolf

Coyote

Eastern wolf

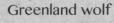 Ethiopian wolf

Golden jackal

Greenland wolf

 Grey wolf

 Black-backed jackal and side-striped jackal

 Red wolf

Today, the wolves' territories are much smaller, but they still adapt easily to very varied environments. They are born survivors.

EUROPE

ASIA

AFRICA

AUSTRALIA

THE WOLF'S PREY

From the bursting buds of summer to the icy depths of winter, the mind of the wolf remains focused on one thing: prey. With an insatiable appetite for meat, wolves are carnivores. As predators at the top of the food chain, their life is a constant quest for the next kill.

Large kills are best, from a hoofed herd. Elk, bison, deer, antelope or moose provide sustenance to last the long winter.

Arctic hares and beavers are small prey, but can prove substantial if found frequently.

When food is scarce, fish, birds, insects, plants, berries and snakes must be enough.

23

THE HUNT

Hearts pounding, ears flicked forward, bodies tensed and eyes flashing fire. The hunt is nearing its end. The pack is one body, one movement, one mind, chasing the thundering hooves until one of the herd separates. Injured, the bison falters and cannot keep up. The pack picks up pace. The gap is closing. Soon they will be upon him, and it will be over.

JAWS OF DEATH

After the hunt, the feasting commences. The wolves feed hungrily on the carcass of the kill, as efficient in eating as they are excellent in hunting. Ferocious teeth and a powerful jaw equip them to extract all they can. No morsel is squandered; no scrap is wasted.

If the captured prey is large, a wolf will eat as much as possible. It can consume 8 kilograms in a single meal, and might survive on this for the next two weeks. Wolves never know when they will eat again.

NECK

A strong, thick neck is perfect for pulling and wrenching meat.

TEETH

Over 40 large, sharp teeth grab and hold prey, tear meat and crunch bone. Wolves have eight molars and four long fangs.

JAW

A mighty jaw, five times as powerful as ours, is ideal for chewing tough flesh. Wolves crack through bones to reach nutritious marrow.

27

ROAMING THE LAND

Silhouetted against the wide sky, they slip, single file, across the frozen lake. Fleet of foot, long-legged and lean, wolves are natural travellers.

Whether crossing a rushing river, scaling an icy peak or stealing swiftly and softly through fresh snow, they keep on the move. Their pack territory spans hundreds of kilometres, and wolves must patrol their land and guard their prey.

Often travelling for 10 hours a day, they keep to a steady pace, accelerating into explosive sprints of up to 65 kilometres per hour when giving chase.

The pack moves onwards, silent and sure-footed.

A toe-to-toe troop of travellers.

A PLACE OF SHELTER

Springtime bluebells blossom. Her pups will soon be here and she must find the perfect spot. Hidden from the eyes of attackers, high enough to keep lookout, close to the gurgle of water. Shaded; protected: the place her new-born pups will be safe for their precious first weeks of life.

Perhaps it will be in a deep cleft between rocks, the hole beneath an upturned tree or a riverbank hollow. It might be a den carved out by wolf mothers before her, or an abandoned beaver dam.

She searches on. When she finds the right place, she will know it.

FIRST FOOTSTEPS

At first, they only know their mother's heartbeat. Six small siblings nestle close for warmth and milk. Her eyes are their eyes. Her ears are their ears.

Soon they peep from the den, their eyes a startling sky-blue. Their parents are hunting, but the pups are never alone. Always watched and guarded by a member of the pack, they take their first shaky steps into the wild world.

Before long, they pad about a new outdoor den. Joyful days are spent chasing their tails, tossing each other bones and yipping with glee. They jab and jostle, roll and tumble. By imitating the adults in their play, they gain strength and skill.

Prized and cherished, the pups are the treasure of the pack.

PUP DEVELOPMENT

Birth
Pups are born after 63 days. They cannot see or hear.

2 weeks
Their eyes are open and the pups begin to walk.

3 weeks
Their milk teeth grow.

6 weeks
The pups take frequent small trips away from the den.

8 weeks
They now eat only solid food. They live and play in a new outdoor den.

10 weeks
The pups grow adult teeth.

12 weeks
They begin travelling and hunting.

33

ENEMIES OF THE WOLF

The wise wolf stays ever light-footed and on its guard.
Ears remain pricked, listening instinctively for danger.
An attack could be close at any time.

RIVAL WOLVES

Rival wolves could make
a deadly stake to territory.

VULTURES

Scavengers lurk, eager to steal
from the wolf's kill.

BROWN BEARS

Brown bears are a fearsome
threat, particularly to the youngest
of the pack. In a fight, they are
formidable opponents.

LIONS AND COYOTES

Mountain lions or coyotes might challenge for prey.

HUMANS

Humans are the most dangerous of all the wolf's enemies.

FRIENDS OF THE WOLF

Not all have lived in fear of the wolf.

Swooping and soaring, the black-winged raven has always followed the wolf. No one knows the language they share. Could the raven offer wolves a sky-high set of eyes and ears, its cry alerting them to prey and danger? Known as the 'wolf-bird', it beats its heavy wings above wolf packs, picking at kills and sweeping at tails in play.

The wolf dances through Native American song and story. These ancient people, so in tune with their surroundings, live in admiration, not fear, of the wolf. They favour its freedom and respect it as a creature with whom to share the richness of the earth. Recognising its part in the natural order, for them the wolf is a symbol of loyalty, strength and courage.

37

THE TWO FACES

Tales of wolves are whispered in all corners of the world. Their wild, untamed spirit breathes into folklore and captures the imagination.

Frequently, they are depicted as tender caregivers, offering protection, shelter and love. The idea of a nurturing wolf has existed for thousands of years.

In Roman mythology we find the story of Romulus and Remus, twin baby brothers sentenced to death by an angry king. The boys are rescued from a basket floating down the River Tiber and are fed, cared for and nursed back to health by a she-wolf. The story goes on to say that one of the boys, Romulus, grows up to be founder of the ancient city of Rome.

A warm, loving wolf pack comes to the rescue in Rudyard Kipling's *The Jungle Book*. In this wonderful collection of tales set in India, Mowgli – the man-cub – is raised by wolves after they discover him lost and alone in the jungle. They adopt him into their pack and seek to protect him from the threat of a man-eating tiger.

 OF THE WOLF

More often, wolves are portrayed as cunning deceivers or bloodthirsty monsters. The Big Bad Wolf who prowls through fairy tales was built on the fears of early farmers. Although attacks on humans were rare, people feared for their livestock and wolves were painted as evil and greedy, preying on the innocent.

A cunning wolf outwits a young girl in the tale of Little Red Riding Hood. A wicked wolf tricks and deceives the girl and her grandmother as he schemes to gobble them both up.

Similarly, the menacing Big Bad Wolf in the story of The Three Little Pigs is determined to devour each of the pigs. He huffs and puffs and tries to destroy their homes in order to catch and eat them.

However, the wolf of fairy tales almost always meets a deadly fate, outsmarted by the hero of the story. Such tales helped to calm fears about real wolves and justify the practice of hunting them down.

When it comes to storytelling, we are drawn to wolves – whether portrayed as good or bad – above all other creatures. The glint in their eye speaks of danger and daring.

HUNTED BY HUMANS

Once, the wild wolf roamed free. He belonged to the land and the land belonged to him.

But as humans have begun to populate more and more of the earth, the wolf's world has changed. Forests have shrunk; the open land is no longer his to wander. Prey is rarer, and the wolf competes for it against hunters.

Those hunters might kill him, too. Hunters ignorant of the wolf's world and who fear he will needlessly attack livestock; hunters who force him from so many homes.

As his land disappears, so does his wolf community.

HOMELANDS OF THE GREY WOLF

Travelling the world and acclimatising quickly to extremes of hot and cold, the grey wolf was once found in more places than any other mammal on earth. Settling wherever prey could be hunted and shelter found, the wolf survived for centuries.

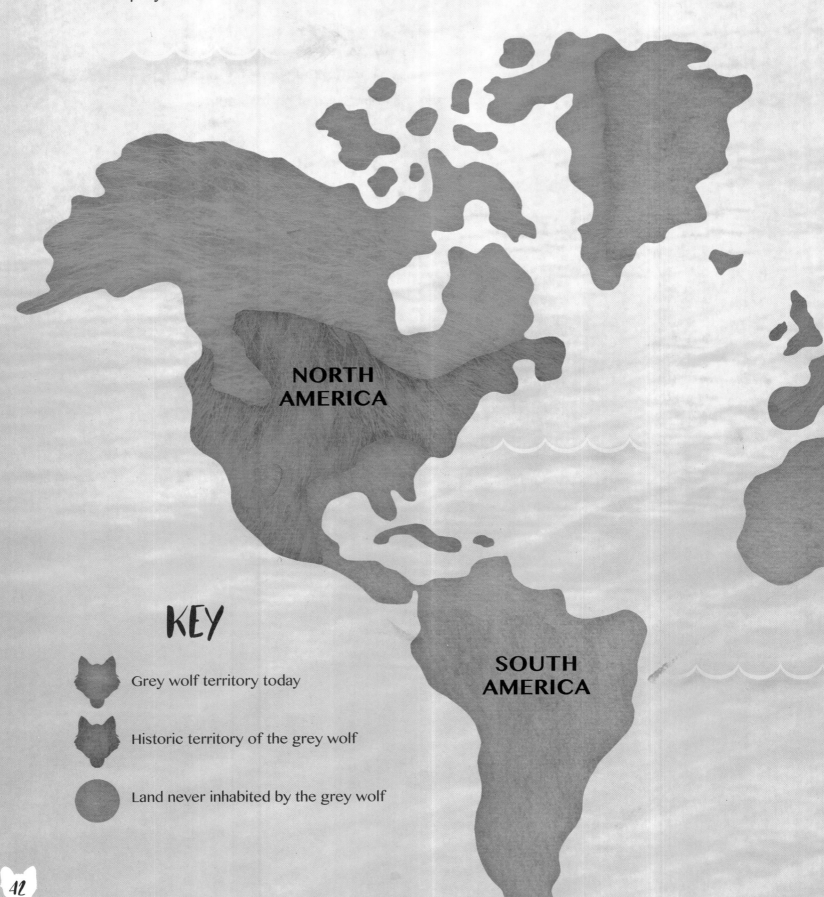

NORTH AMERICA

SOUTH AMERICA

KEY

Grey wolf territory today

Historic territory of the grey wolf

Land never inhabited by the grey wolf

But a great danger crept up: people. Humans chopped down forests to make their homes, and fear drove them to hunt and destroy the wolf. Today, it is only in smaller parts of North America, Europe and Asia that wolves are found, much reduced in number, hiding in the shadows.

EUROPE

ASIA

AFRICA

AUSTRALIA

THE SURVIVAL OF THE WOLF

Finally, after centuries of wolf-hunting, several countries have passed laws to protect these magnificent creatures. Promisingly, it is now recognised that wolves help to maintain a balanced ecosystem, playing their own role in preserving the life of plants and animals in their surrounding area. Efforts to reintroduce wolves to their old habitats are now underway.

MISLEADING MYTHS

WOLVES NEED TO KILL HUMANS

Wolves are shy creatures that are afraid of humans.
They are likely to run away when confronted.

WOLVES KILL FOR FUN

Like other predators, wolves kill prey to ensure their own
survival. They target the weak, injured, young or old members
of a herd. These are least likely to fight back or cause injury.
Only one hunt out of 10 will result in a kill.

WOLVES ARE UNNECESSARY PESTS

Wolves are part of a balanced, healthy and sustainable
ecosystem. By picking off weaker animals, they
help to keep herds healthy and strong.

WOLVES ARE SAVAGE

Wolves share many of our human characteristics:
they are often playful and affectionate, and
they are deeply tied by family bonds.

HELP WOLVES TO THRIVE

Do you want to help wolves to survive? You can:

- Find out as much as you can about wolves
- Be environmentally friendly, to save the habitats of wolves
- Help others to discover the truth about wolves and their wild and wonderful ways

One of the best ways to find out about wolves is through wolf conservation groups. These organisations work to protect wild wolves and their habitats. In the UK, you could reach out to the **UK Wolf Conservation Trust**. It helps to educate the public about wolves, raises money to fund wolf conservation projects around the world and provides opportunities for scientists to research wolves. You can visit their site in southern England, which is home to 10 wolves, or you can visit their website: **www.ukwolf.org**.

INDEX